A is for Arch

A St. Louis Alphabet

Barbara Forrest

ISBN 9780578553856

Published in the United States by Watercolor Press

for Rob

husband, best friend,

partner in art and life

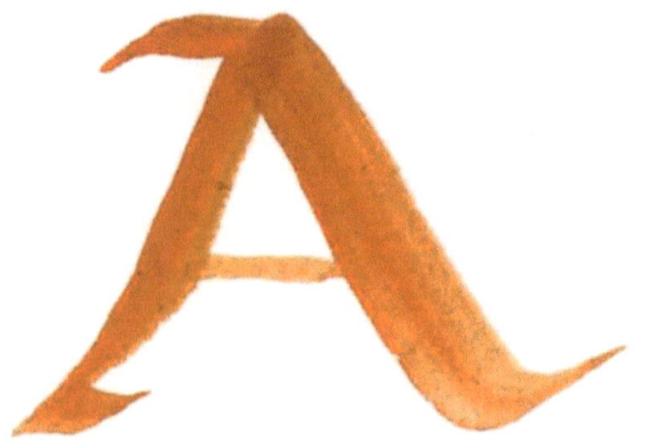

is for

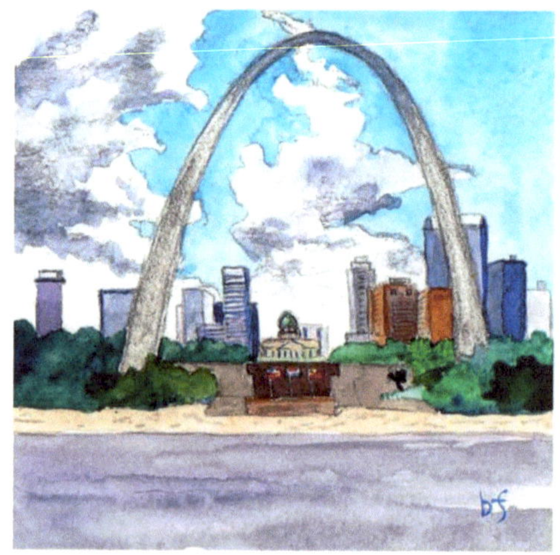

Arch

Soaring above the riverfront, the Gateway Arch
is THE iconic symbol of St. Louis.
It is spectacular.

B

is for

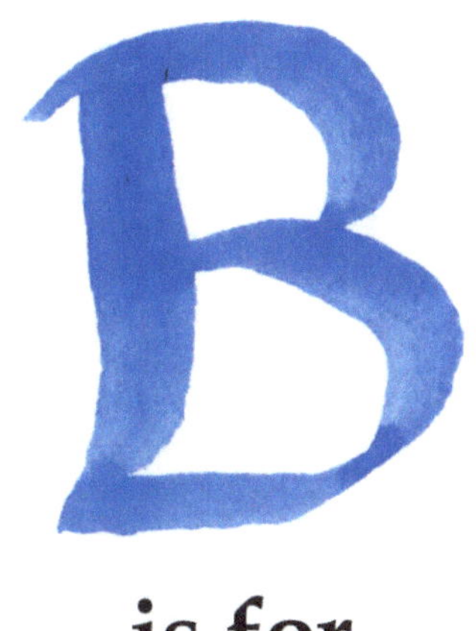

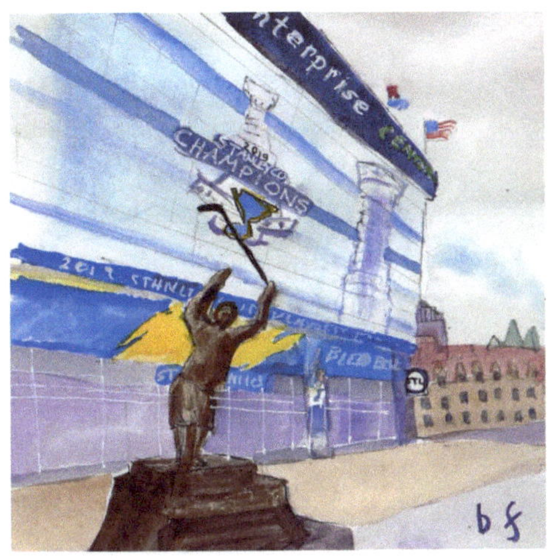

Blues

In 2019, the Blues did the impossible.
They went from last to best,
winning their first Stanley Cup.

C

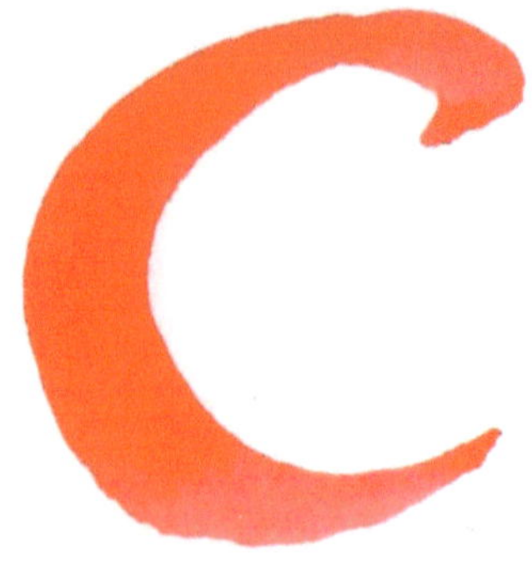

is for

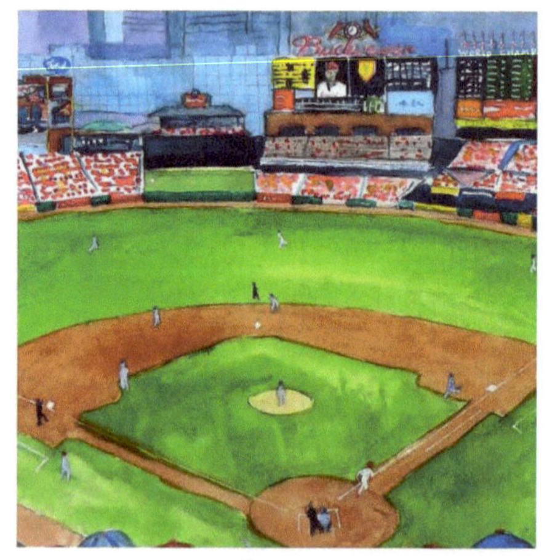

Cardinals

Fans are passionate about their St. Louis Cardinals,
winners of 11 World Series titles.

D

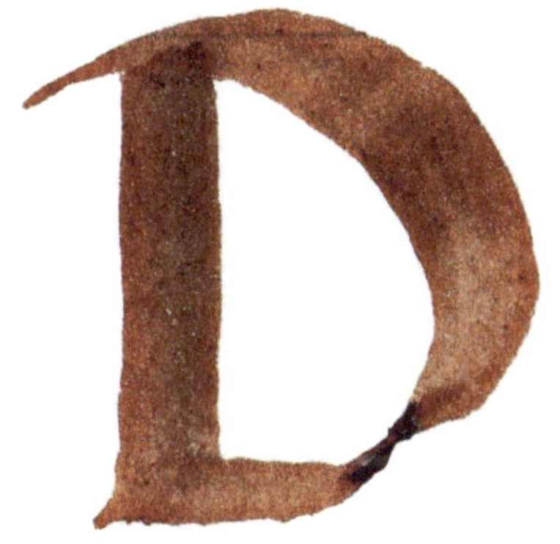

is for

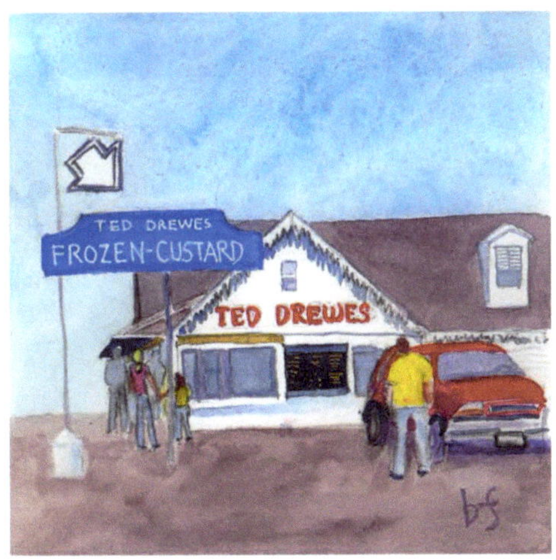

Ted Drewes

Ted Drewes is a famous frozen custard stand, operated by the same family since 1929.

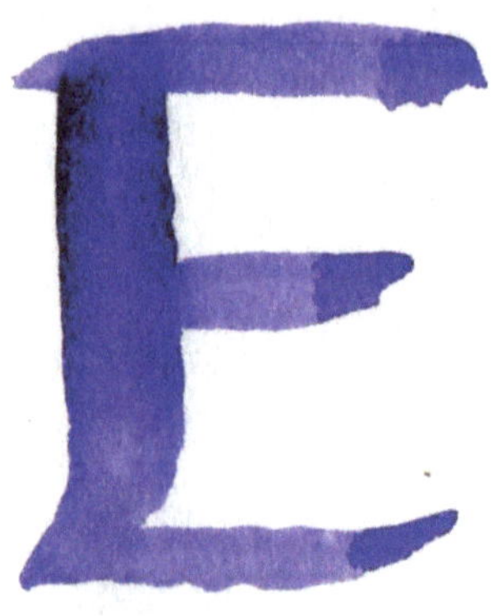

is for

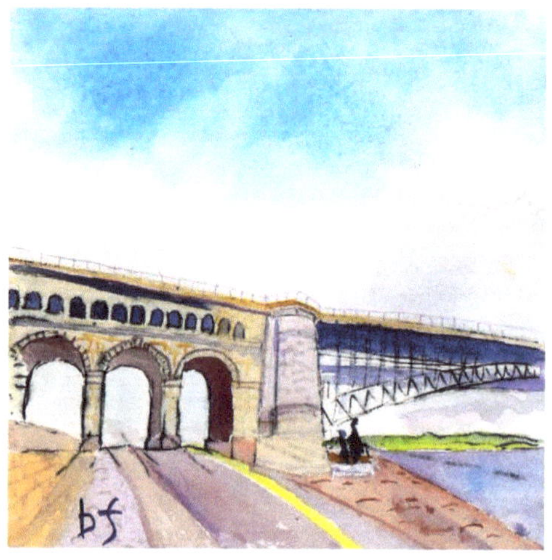

Eads Bridge

The Eads Bridge was an engineering marvel when it was first built in 1874 and still carries folks across the Mississippi River today.

F

is for

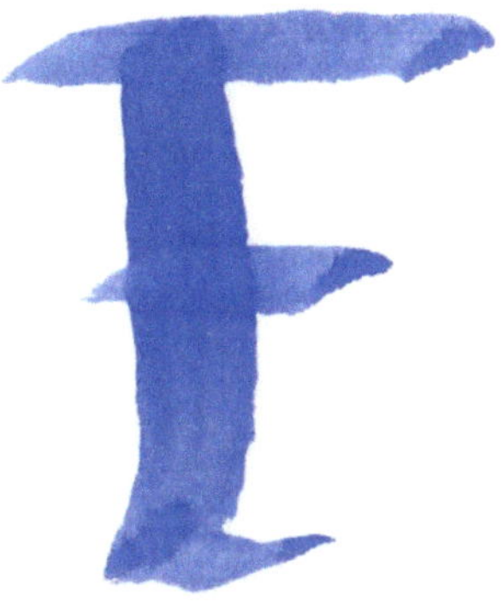

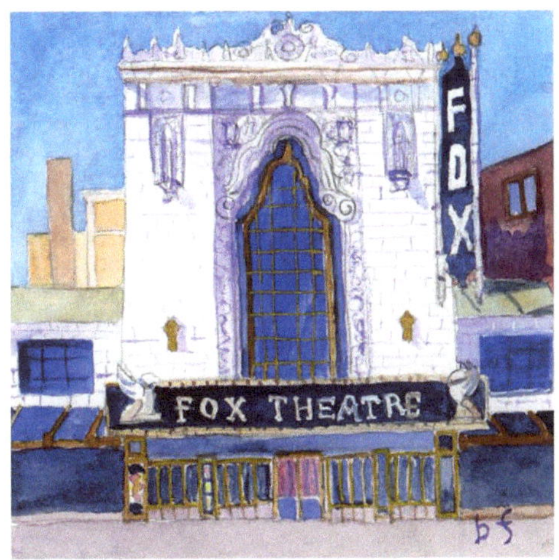

Fox

The Fox Theatre opened in 1929 and
the extravagant interior is something to behold.

G

is for

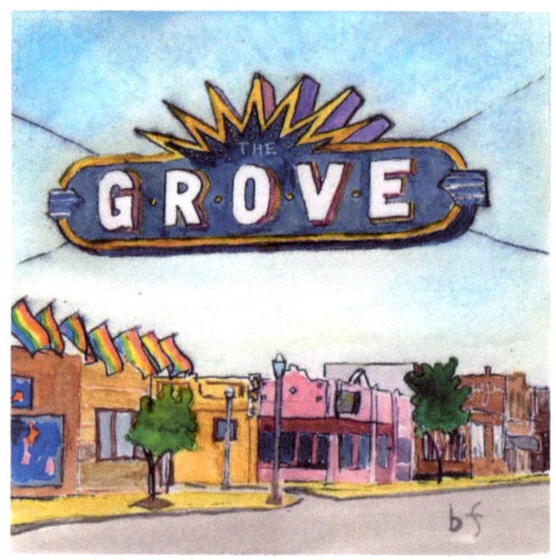

the Grove

The Grove is a diverse neighborhood
with lots of nightlife.

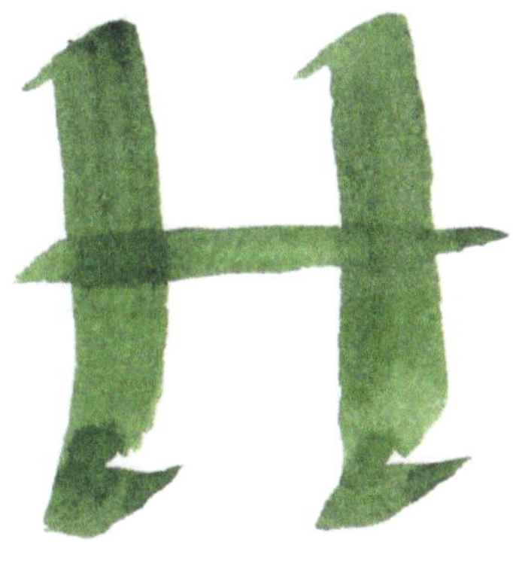

is for

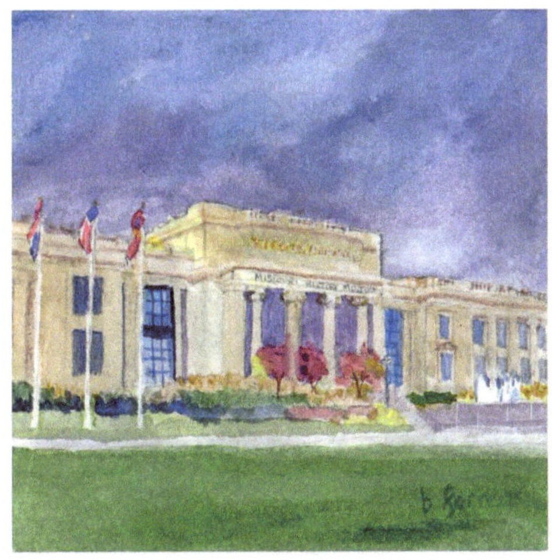

History Museum

The Missouri History Museum has fascinating
exhibits which celebrate the past and present.

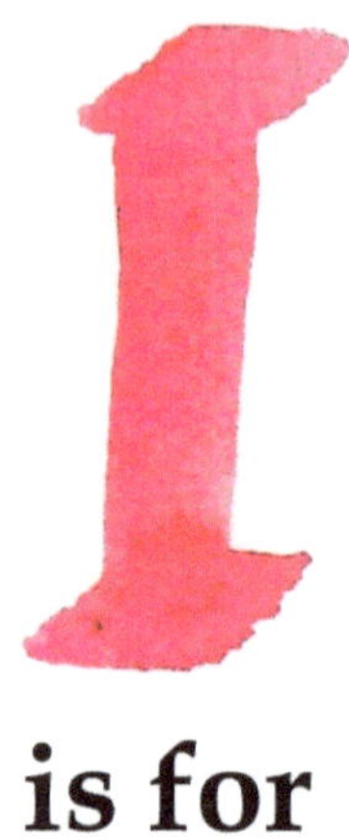

is for

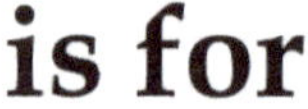

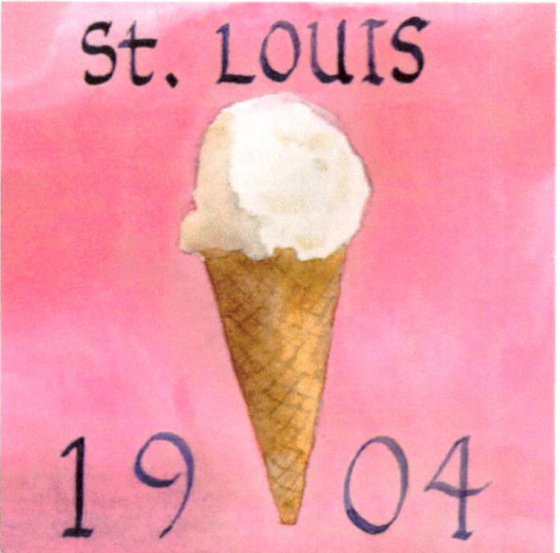

Ice Cream

Local lore claims that the ice cream cone
was invented at the 1904
St. Louis World's Fair.

J

is for

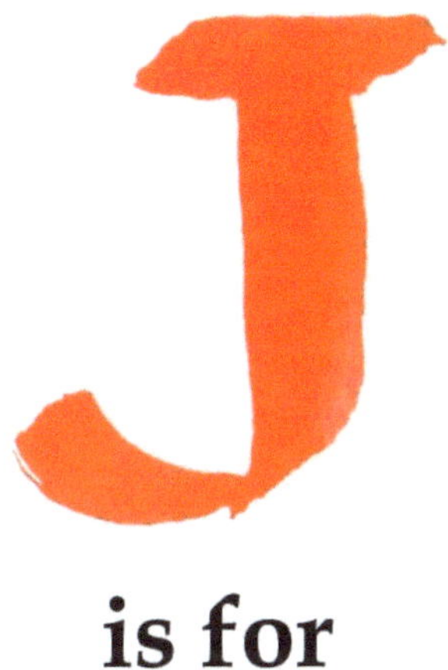

Japanese Garden

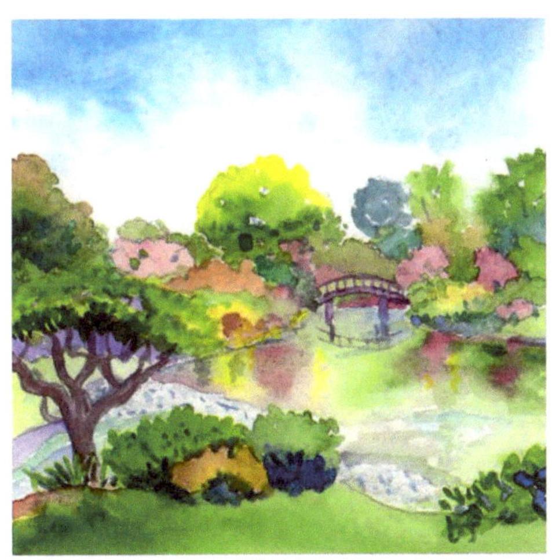

The Japanese Garden is part of the
huge and fascinating Missouri Botanical Garden.

K

is for

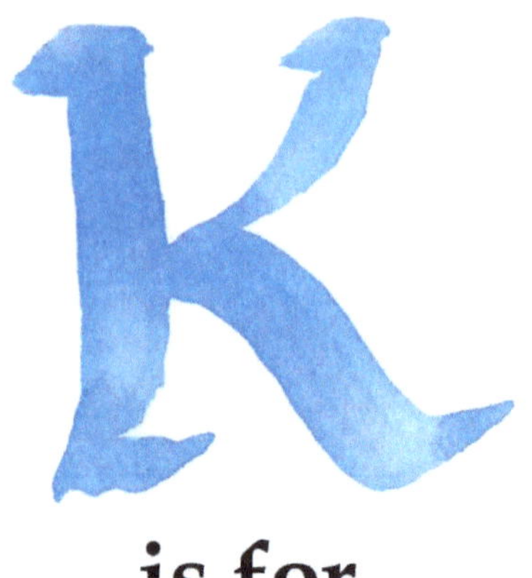

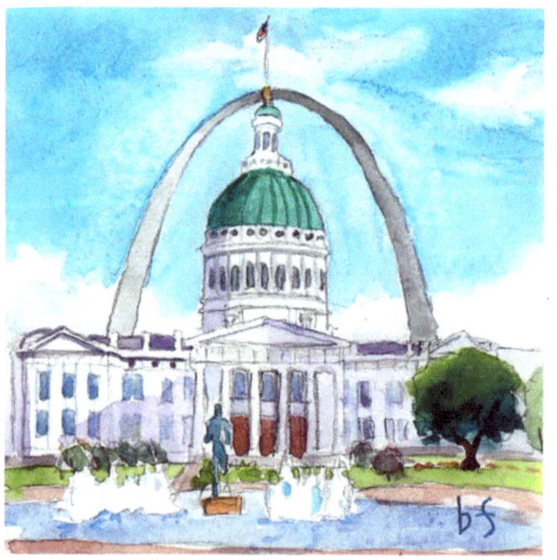

Kiener Plaza

**Gatherings. Protests. Celebrations. Marches.
It's all happening at Kiener Plaza.**

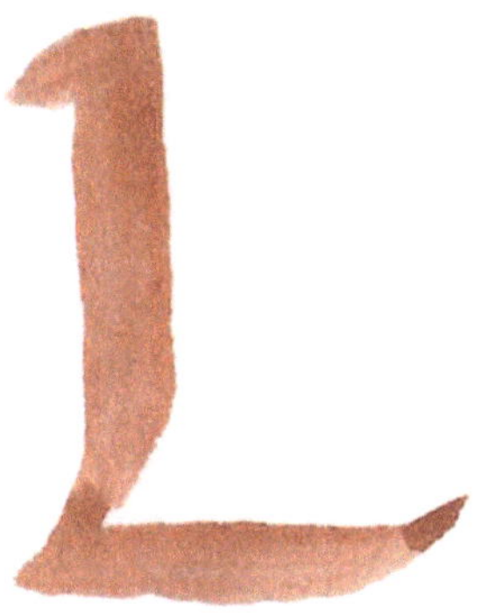

is for

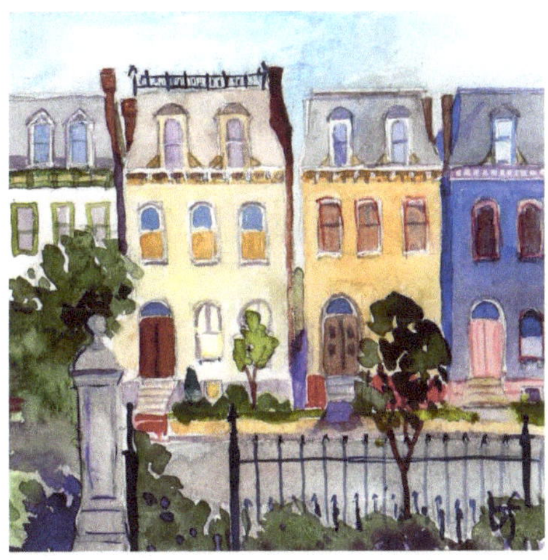

Lafayette Square

Lafayette Square is a beautiful restored
Victorian neighborhood in St. Louis,
which surrounds a historic park.

M

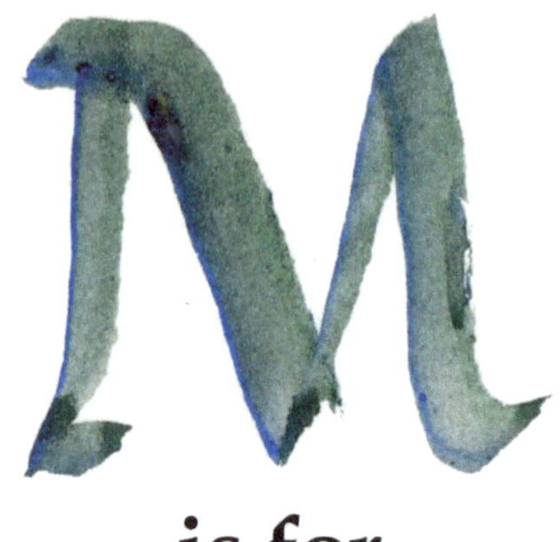

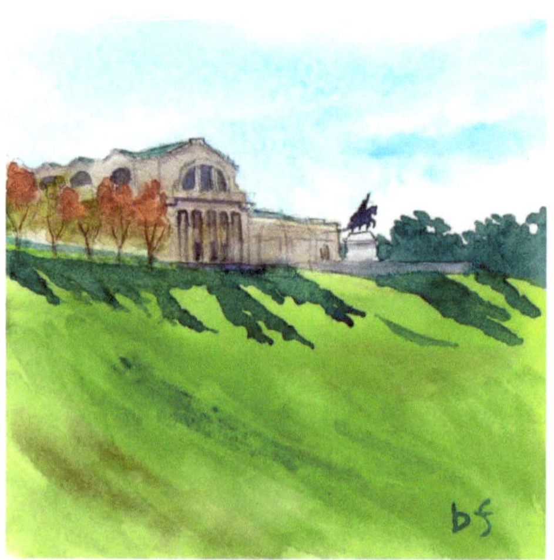

Art Museum

The St. Louis Art Museum is world class.
Etched in stone on the front is
"Dedicated to Art and Free to All".

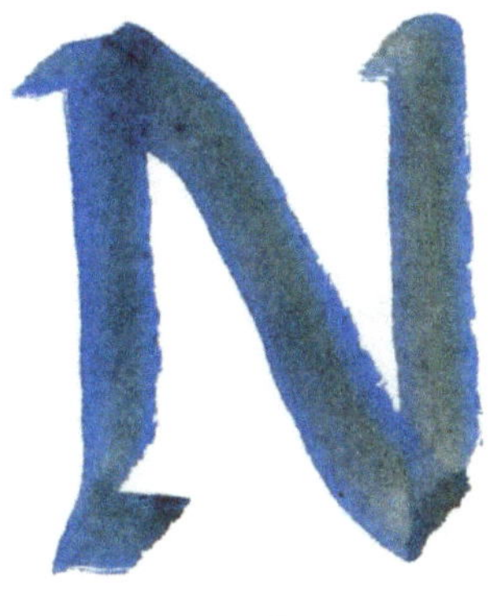

is for

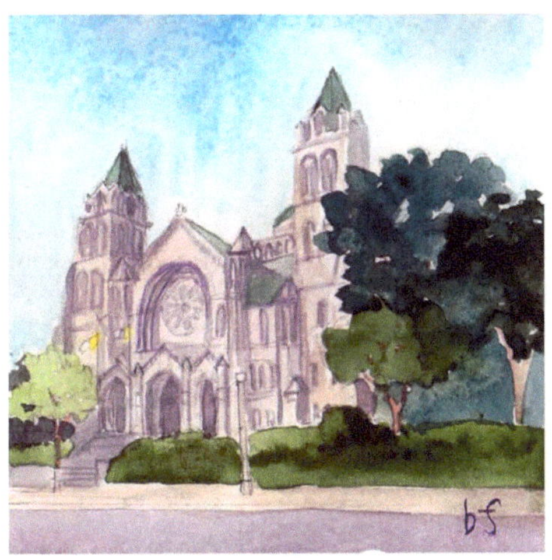

New Cathedral

The Cathedral Basilica of Saint Louis
is a mosaic filled wonder. It was completed in 1914
but folks still call it the New Cathedral.

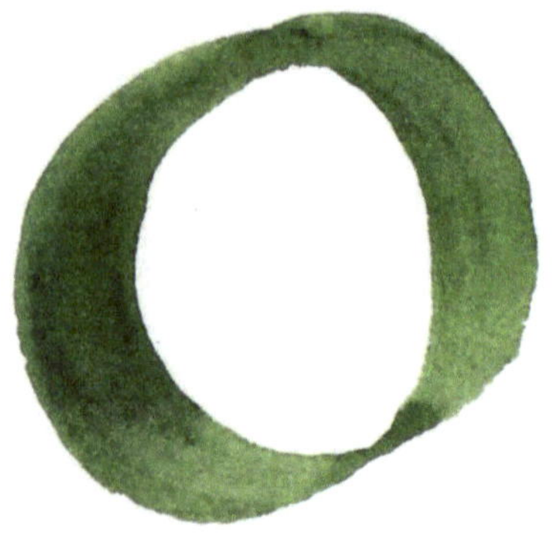

is for

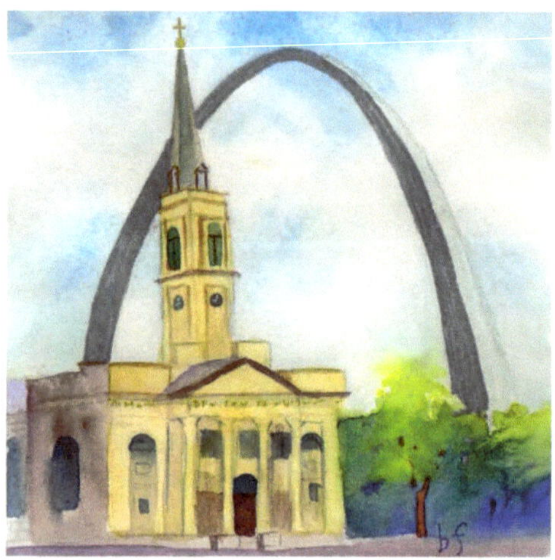

Old Cathedral

The Old Cathedral, standing in the shadow of the Gateway Arch, is the oldest building in St. Louis, begun in 1831.

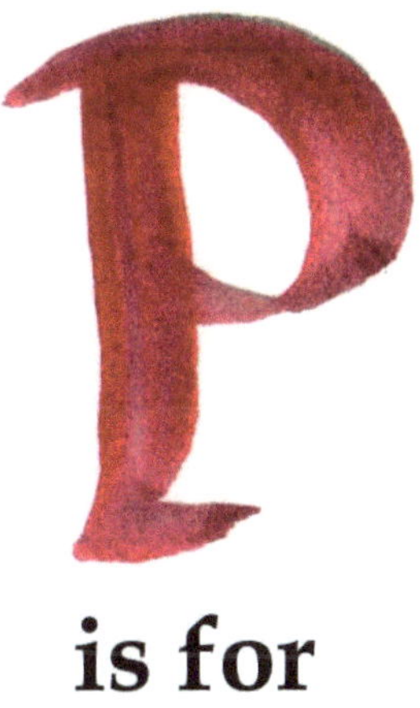

is for

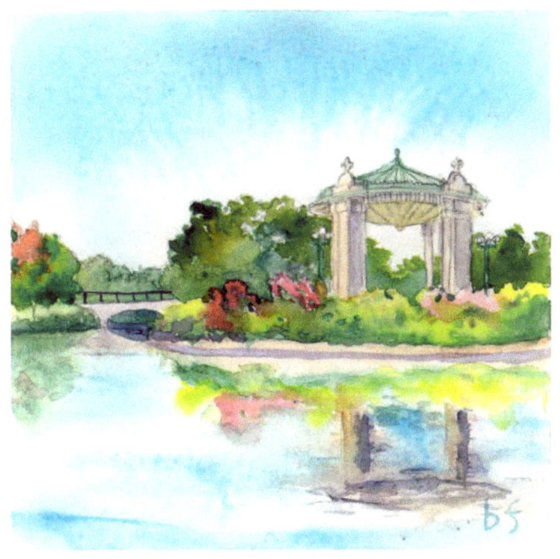

Forest Park

One of the greatest treasures of St. Louis,
Forest Park contains the Zoo, several museums,
the Muny Opera, and endless recreation opportunities.

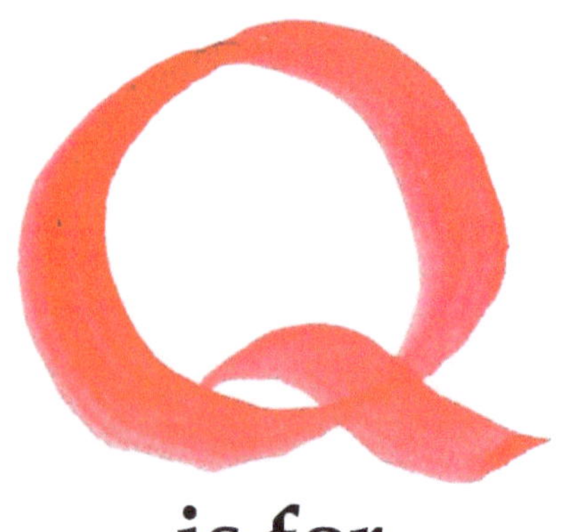

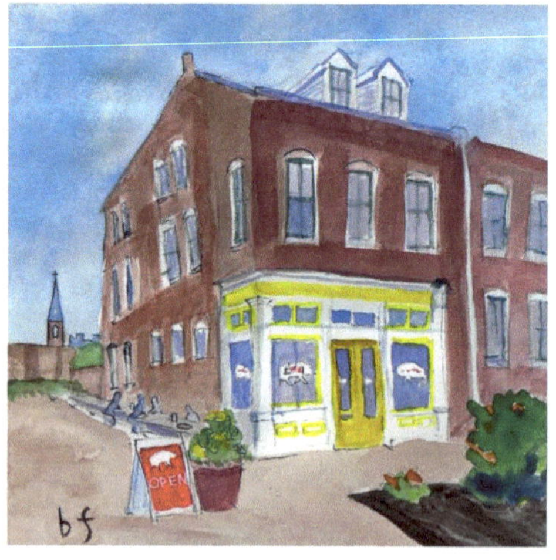

Q as in BBQ

St. Louis is justifiably famous for
its barbeque. Ribs, brisket and links..
all good! You can just call it "Q"

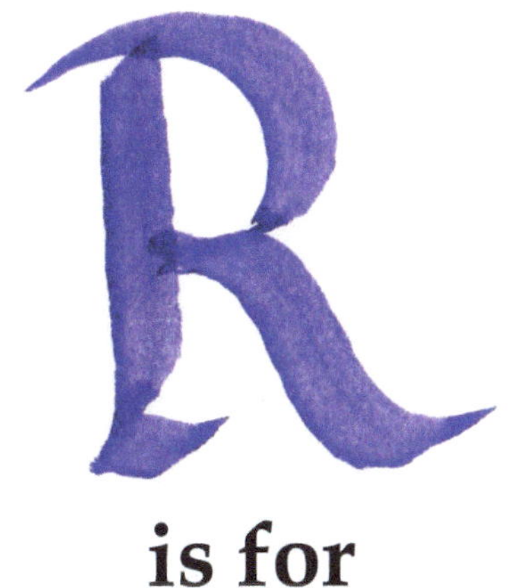

is for

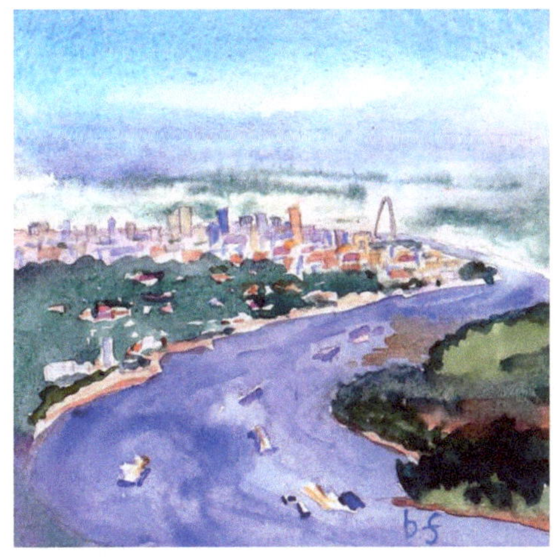

Mississippi River

The River is why St. Louis exists.
It's part of our history and our present.

S

is for

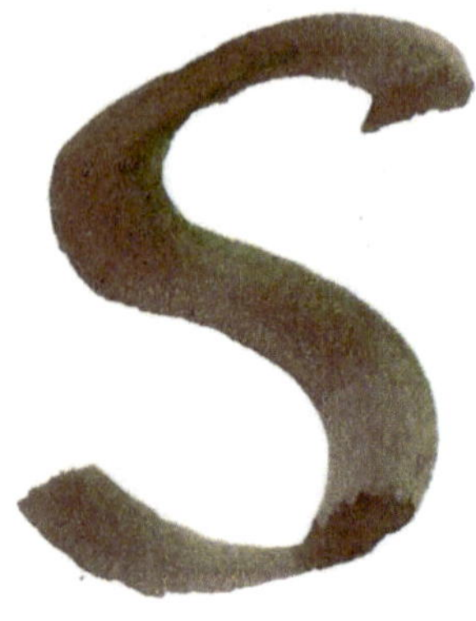

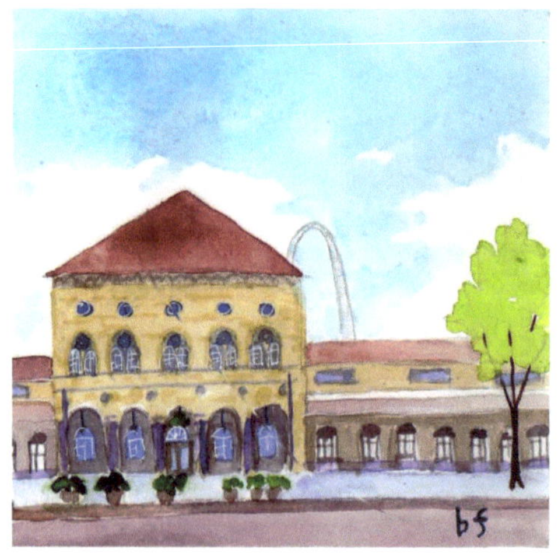

Soulard

This old neighborhood is home to the
Soulard Farmer's Market, established in 1779.

T

is for

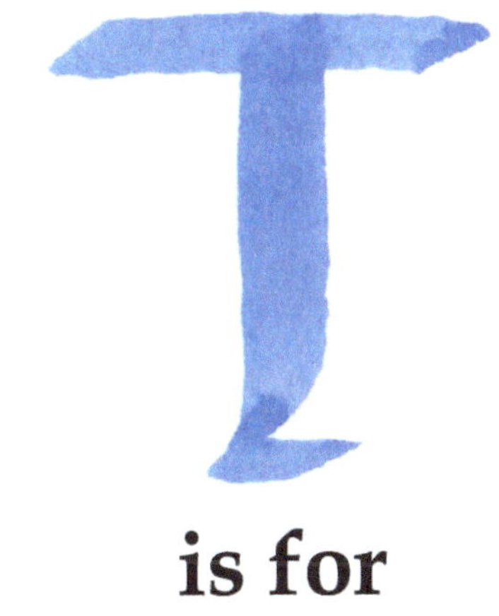

Tower Grove Park

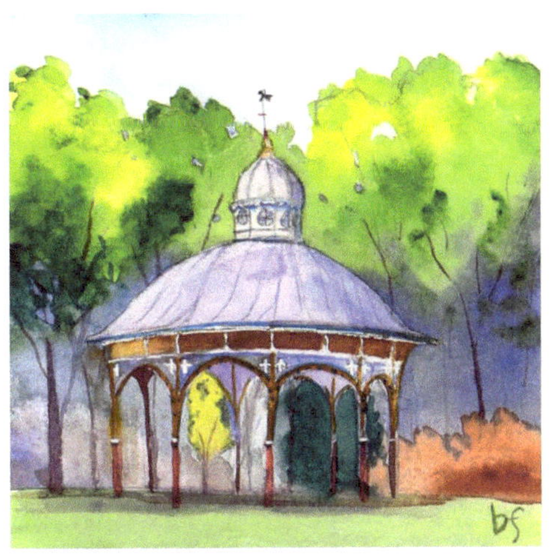

Founded in 1868, Tower Grove is a wooded
Victorian park with grassy meadows, pavilions,
and recreational and cultural venues.

is for

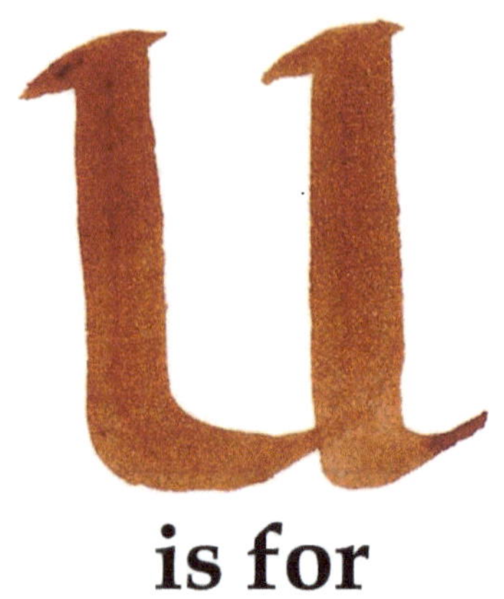

Union Station

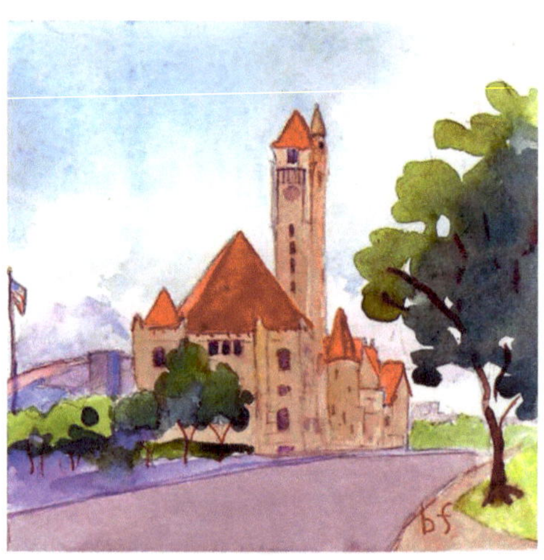

Union Station, built in 1892, was once one
of the busiest passenger rail terminals in the world.
Now the Grand Hall is a fabulous hotel lobby and lounge.

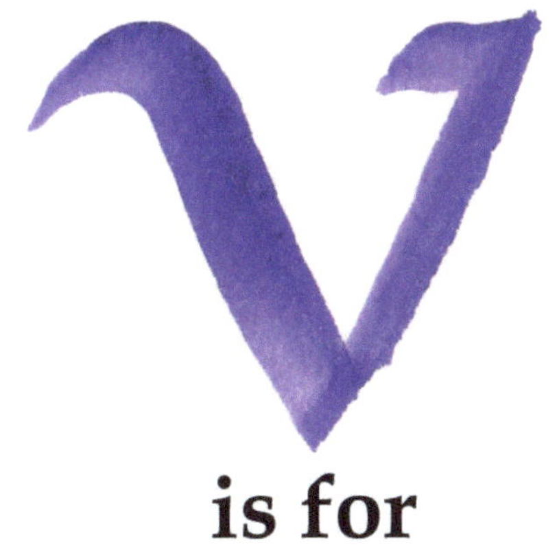

is for

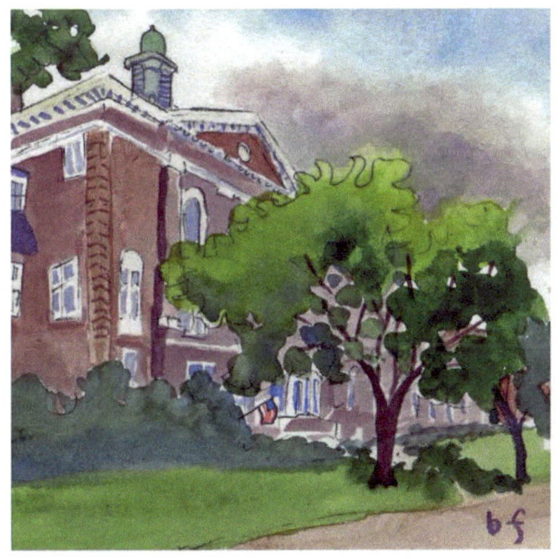

the Ville

The Ville is a historic African-American neighborhood. Sumner High School (pictured above) alumni include Arthur Ashe and Chuck Berry.

W

is for

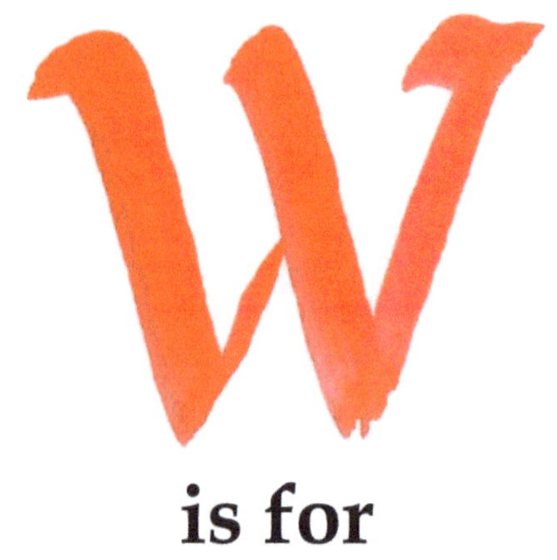

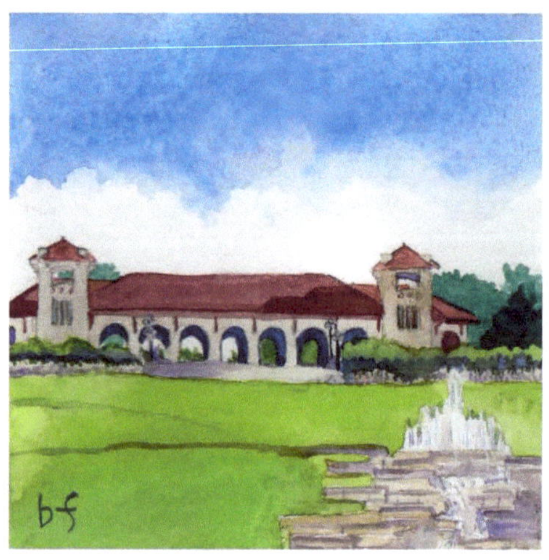

World's Fair Pavilion

Built in 1909, this open air pavilion is one
of the many impressive structures in Forest Park.

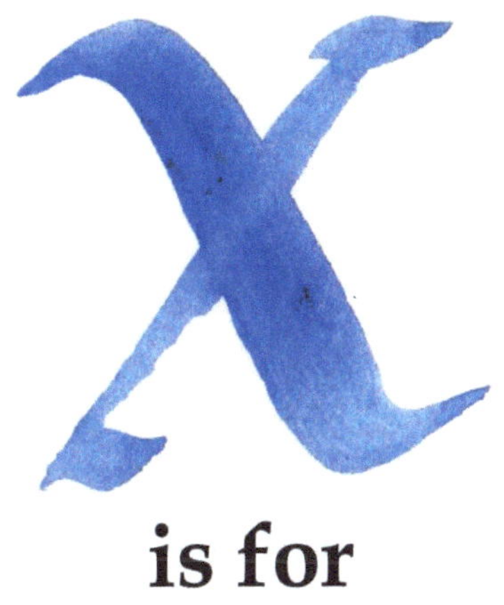

is for

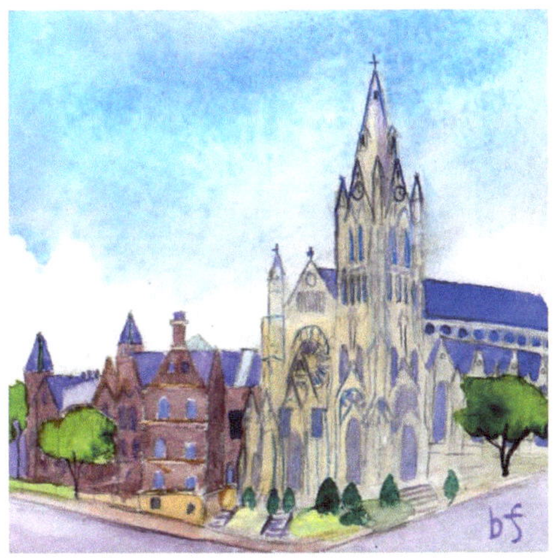

St. Francis Xavier College Church

This soaring church sits on the campus of Saint Louis University. It is particularly beautiful when lit up at night.

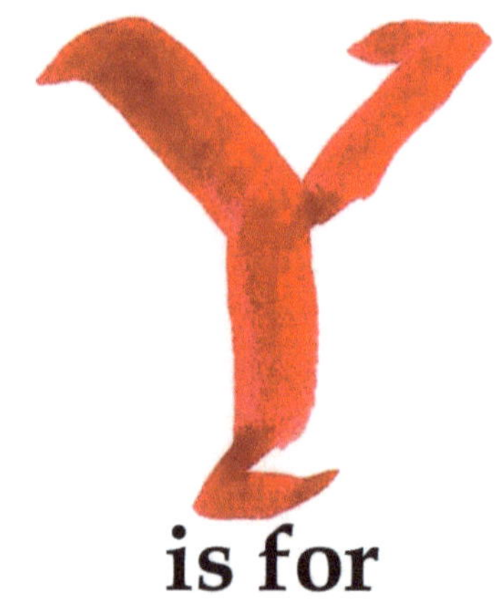

is for

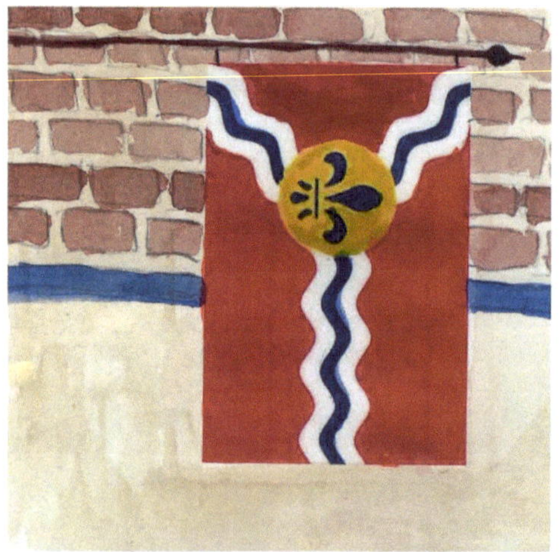

the Y
in our flag

The wavy blue lines represent the confluence of
the Mississippi and Missouri Rivers.
It's a great looking flag.

Z

is for

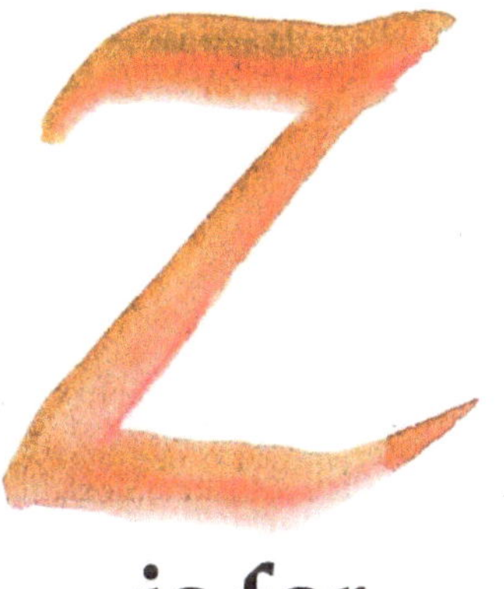

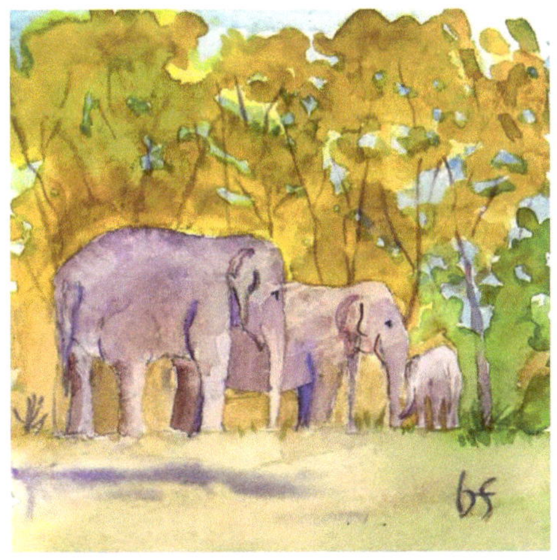

Zoo

Another very popular attraction in Forest Park,
the St. Louis Zoo is world famous...and free.

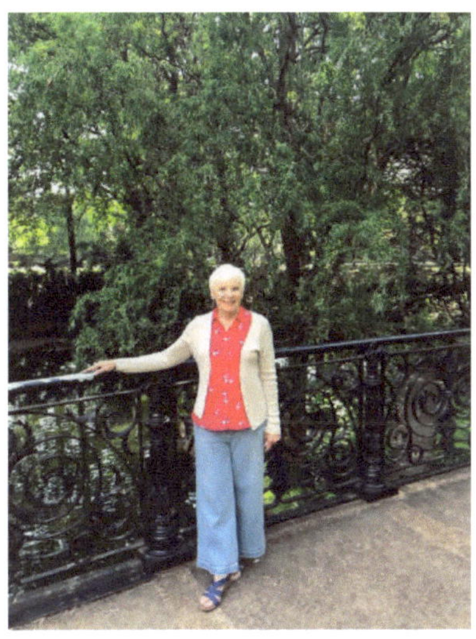

ABOUT THE AUTHOR/ARTIST

Born in St. Louis, Barbara Forrest found her way back to her native city via a wandering journey which led her to Texas, Canada, Oregon and Colorado. She was always sketching and painting as a child, and now has been making her living as an artist since 1998. She specializes in watercolor landscapes which can range in size from 3" x 3" to 3 x 4 ft.

An avid hiker, she will go to the distance to get just the right composition for a painting. Barbara's goal is that her work expresses the joy she finds in both nature and painting.

Barbara's work is represented in galleries and shops throughout Oregon, Arizona, Colorado, Hawaii and on her website, forrestgallery.net